PHILIPPIANS

DAN NICHOLS

PRESS

Published by StoryBuilders Press
eBook: 978-1-954521-66-7
Paperback: 978-1-954521-67-4

To Landon and Declan

I love you more than you'll ever know!

Dan Nichols has provided us with something that's missing, a biblical paraphrase aimed at kids who are too old for children's books and too young for adult vocabulary. I'm a big fan of anything that gets God's Word into the hands and hearts of our youth. Thank you, Dan!

Dr. Larry Osborne
North Coast Church
Teaching Pastor & Kingdom Ambassador

What a wonderful, creative, and fun way to communicate the truths of Philippians! It's exciting to think of seeing younger ones learning what Paul the apostle was writing in a way that they can grasp and understand.

Dan Kimball
Vice-President of Western Seminary
Author, *How (Not) to Read the Bible*

What a great tool to help encourage young hearts to study the Bible! Dan's desire to see the Gospel read and understood by young Christ followers exemplifies the Father heart of God. Teaching the next generation how to utilize their spiritual sword may be the greatest gift we can leave them.

Rachel Benjamin
Writer for The Skit Guys

I am constantly looking for tools to help me invest in the spiritual development of my grandkids. I love Making Scripture Simple, *not only because it makes Scripture understandable, but also includes great questions that create meaningful conversations. I am excited to use this awesome resource.*

Lance Witt
Founder, Replenish Ministries

One of God's great gifts in Dan Nichols is his ability to creatively and memorably communicate the truth of God's Word. In Making Scripture Simple, *he has brought Philippians into a format that helps kids connect with Scripture so they can understand how it applies to their life. Such a valuable tool in shaping the hearts of the next generation!*

Nancy Moore
Founder, N.L. Moore & Associates

One of my greatest hopes is that my four kids grow up to have a genuine love and true walk with Jesus. To that end, Dan has created a thoughtful gift that can help us draw near to God's Word with our kids. If you are looking to jump-start or rekindle intentional time together—this is it.

Pat Linnell
Founder, Grace Bomb

WHAT'S THE BIBLE ALL ABOUT?

*T*he Bible is the best-selling book of all time for a reason...because it's not just another book. It's actually a collection of sixty-six books originally written over 1,500+ years by forty different authors on three continents in three languages with one main message: *the Hope of Jesus!* The Bible shows us that Jesus is King, and his love changes everything. The first half of the Bible (the Old Testament) points forward to Jesus. The second half of the Bible (the New Testament) points back to Jesus and all that he accomplished to bring us back to God.

This isn't just a book of myths and legends. This is a book that answers all of humanity's deepest questions regarding origin, purpose, identity, design, and destiny. It's also a book we can trust. As Dr. Voddie Baucham says, "The Bible is a reliable collection of historical documents written by eyewitnesses during the lifetimes of other eyewitnesses. They report to us supernatural events in fulfillment of specific prophecies and claim that their writings are divine rather than human in origin."

The goal of *Making Scripture Simple* is that you and your kids will experience the life-transforming joy, wisdom, beauty, truth, and purpose that God's gift of Scripture was meant to give through *the Hope of Jesus*!

WHAT IS THE HOPE OF JESUS?

*E*very human needs hope, but most people are looking for it in all the wrong places. The One, True God is the only person who can give us real hope that lasts for a lifetime (and beyond). God originally created everything that exists perfectly, but he also gave humanity free will that we've always used to try to *become* our own gods rather than enjoy the Real God. We all start our lives running from God, not towards God.

But John 3:16 gives us good news: "God loved the world so much that he gave his only Son Jesus, that whoever believes in him will never die, but instead have everlasting life." Jesus lived the perfect life that we could never live. He died the death we all deserve for our rebellion against God. And then Jesus destroyed death by coming out of his tomb.

The Hope of Jesus means that anyone can have a restored relationship with God by believing in the perfect life, death and resurrection of Jesus and making him the Lord and Leader of their lives. As you read *Making Scripture Simple*, my hope is that you and your family will embrace *the Hope of Jesus* for yourselves!

HOW TO USE THIS BOOK

*W*hen my son Landon was eight years old, he looked at his mom Joy, and said, "Mom, you know what I think the hardest thing in the world is?"

"No…what?" Joy replied.

"Following Jesus," Landon said.

"Why's that?" asked Joy.

"Because there are so many people who *don't* follow Jesus…" Landon explained.

That same night as I tucked Landon into bed and discussed this with him, I recognized just how deeply he wrestles with his faith and his spiritual life at such a young age.

Maybe you are an elementary or middle school student who's in the same boat as my son Landon.

Maybe that kid is your kid too! Or maybe you're an adult who hasn't really engaged Scripture for yourself, but you'd like to.

Making Scripture Simple is a helpful paraphrase of the Bible that is both engaging for younger students and accessible for adults. Please carve out some time for courageous conversations with your family using the discussion questions in this book. Mark it up! Highlight, underline, circle, dig in, interact, and really take to heart the life-changing *Hope of Jesus* for yourselves.

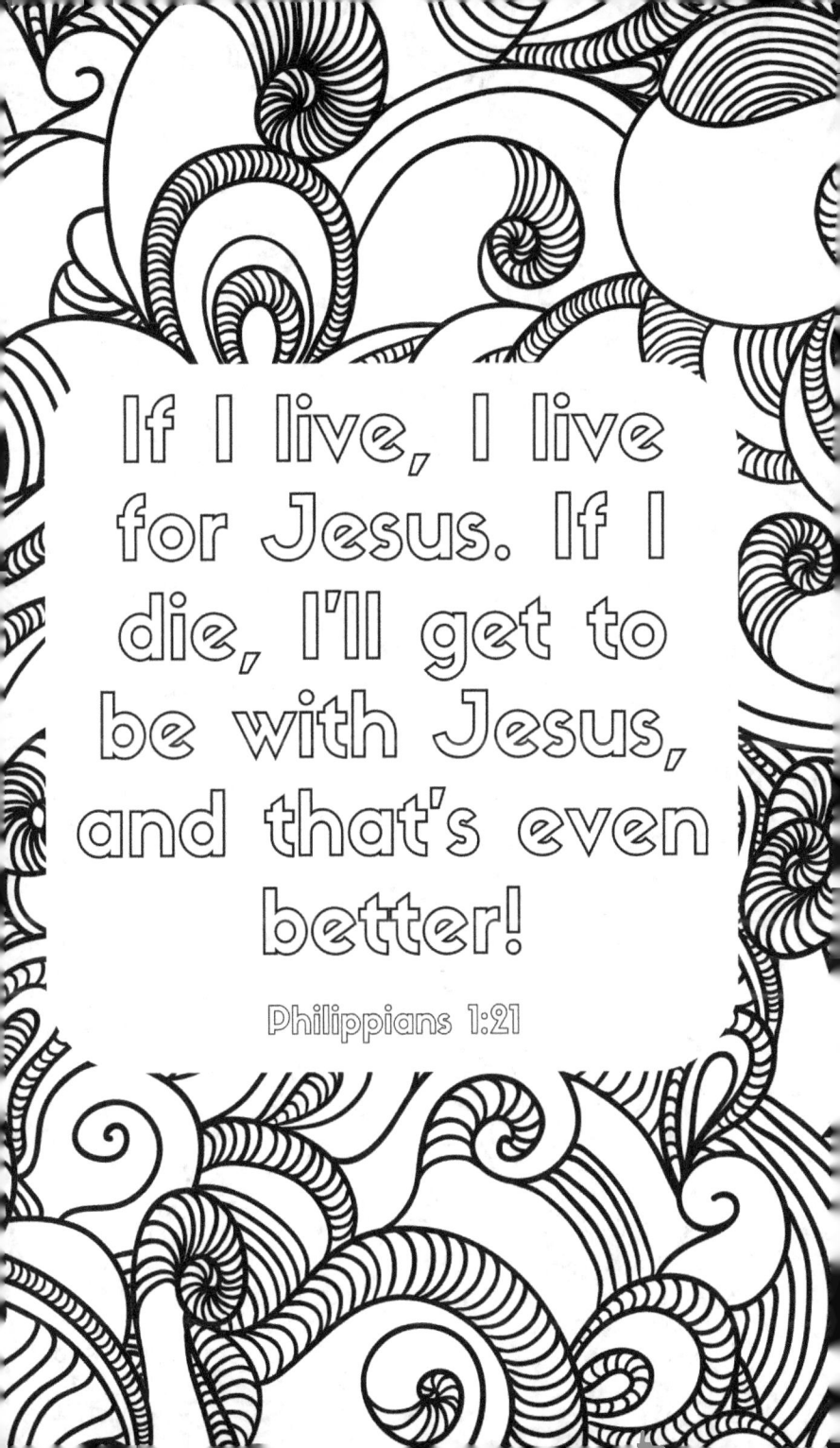

If I live, I live for Jesus. If I die, I'll get to be with Jesus, and that's even better!

Philippians 1:21

CHAPTER
1

Hey Philippians,

1:1 This letter is from Paul and Timothy.

> If you read chapter 16 in Doctor Luke's letter (Acts), you'll remember how we met and all the CRAZY stuff we went through to help you find and follow Jesus.

I'm writing to everyone in Philippi who gave their life to Jesus, and the leaders of your church too – the pastors and deacons.

1:2 I want you to get God's free gifts that you don't deserve, and I want you to have the stability that only God (the best dad) and his son Jesus can give.

1:3 I'm so thankful for you, Philippians!

1:4-5 When I pray for each of you, I'm really happy because we've been teammates for Jesus and his Good News ever since we first met (about ten years ago).

QUESTION?

Who is a friend or family member that you can pray for today like Paul prayed for the Philippians? (Vs. 4-5, 9)

1:6 King Jesus will finish the good work he started in you when he comes back to make everything right again with a New Heaven and a New Earth.

1:7 Feeling this way about you makes sense because we're a close, spiritual family who has gone through really tough stuff together.

1:8 God knows how much I love you like Jesus does!

1:9 And I'm praying that you will love God and others so much more every day.

1:10 This way you'll discover what really matters in

life…what the good life actually is.

The best life is when we keep doing the next right thing until Jesus comes back.

Your personal relationship with Jesus will create character that lasts.

QUESTION❓

What does it mean to do "the next right thing?"
How will you do that today or this week?
(Vs. 10)

1:11 This is spiritual fruit that makes God look great.

1:12 And here's another thing you should know: all the pain I'm going through is helping others hear about the rescue mission of Jesus!

1:13 All the Roman soldiers guarding me here know that I'm under house arrest because I'm spreading the Hope of Jesus everywhere I go.

1:14 And many more followers of Jesus are getting

the courage and confidence to tell others about Christ without being scared!

QUESTION ?

Who is a friend or family member that needs a relationship with Jesus? Have *you* given your life to Jesus yet? (Vs. 12-14)

1:15 Now, some people talk about Jesus for bad reasons (because they're jealous and competitive). But other people talk about Jesus for the right reasons...

1:16 Those people really love me, and they know God picked me to explain why the Good News about Jesus is true.

1:17 But those jealous and competitive people don't talk about Jesus for the right reasons because they're all about themselves.

They aren't trustworthy, and they actually want my house arrest to be more painful for me.

1:18 That's not a big deal, though, because I'm happy that the hope of Jesus is spreading whether people talk about him for the right reasons or not.

1:19 And I know that the Holy Spirit (God living inside us) will help me through your prayers.

1:20 Just like I've been bold for Jesus in the past, I'm going to keep living my life boldly so that Jesus looks great. And it doesn't matter how long I live…

1:21 If I live, I live for Jesus. If I die, I'll get to be with Jesus – and that's even better!

QUESTION ?

Why was Paul not afraid to die?
(Vs. 21-22, 27)

1:22 But if I live, I can help more people find and follow Jesus…so I'm not really sure which option is better.

1:23 I really want to be in Heaven with Jesus, which would be the best thing for *me*.

1:24 But the best thing for all of *you* is that I keep living here on earth.

1:25 Since that's true, I'm confident that God will keep me alive longer so that I can help all of you get closer to Christ and enjoy living for him.

1:26 When I come to spend more time with you there in person, you'll be really proud of how Jesus is using my life for the things that matter most.

1:27 But most importantly, Philippians, always remember that Heaven is your ultimate home, and you are citizens of God's Kingdom first.

This way (whether we see each other again or not) I'll know that you are unified, heading in the same direction together, and standing up for the Good News of Jesus.

1:28 Don't be scared by people who hate you because they don't love Jesus. Your courage will remind them that their future is scary, but your future is secure in God's love.

1:29 Not only does God give you the honor of being part of his forever family, but God gives you the honor of feeling pain for him too.

1:30 And when you suffer, remember: you are not alone, and we're in this together!

You've already watched me go through really hard times in the past, and you're still watching me fight through tough times now.

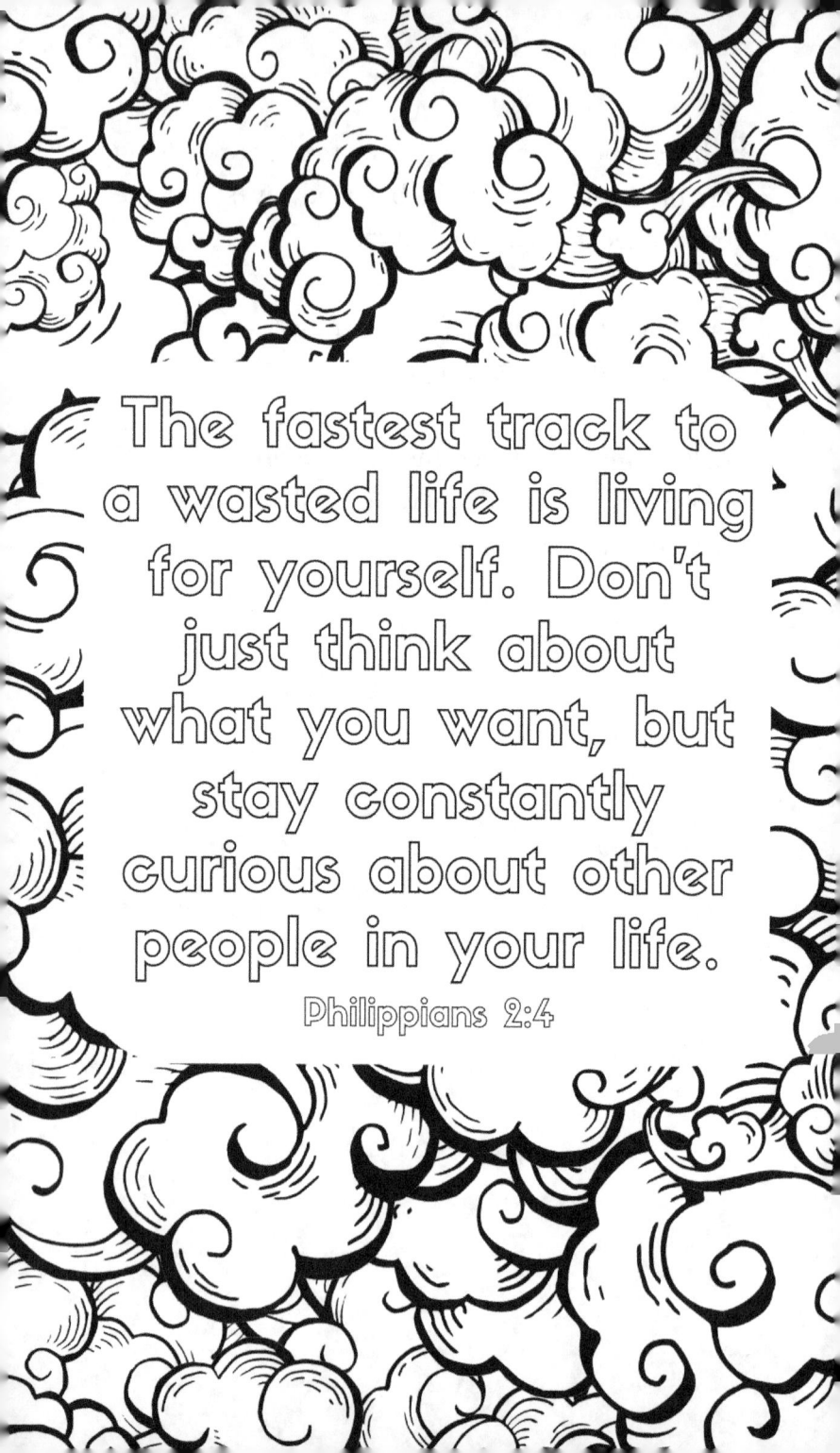

The fastest track to a wasted life is living for yourself. Don't just think about what you want, but stay constantly curious about other people in your life.

Philippians 2:4

CHAPTER
2

2:1 Doesn't a relationship with Jesus encourage you? Doesn't his love make you feel safe? Don't you have more Christian teammates because God lives inside you through the Holy Spirit? Don't you really care about other people now?

2:2 Then make my day by getting along with each other! Sacrifice for each other, and team up together well.

2:3 Don't live for yourself. Don't worry about what others think about you. Think about yourself less, and treat others like they're more important than you are.

2:4 The fastest track to a wasted life is living for yourself. Don't just think about what you want, but stay constantly curious about other people in your life.

QUESTION ❓

Why is it so hard to "treat others like they're more important than you are?" (Vs. 3-4)

2:5 Think about life the same way that Jesus did.

2:6 Even though Jesus is God, he restricted his God-ness to accomplish his mission to save us when he came to earth.

2:7 Jesus came to earth as a humble servant, totally human (without any sin) and totally God at the same time!

2:8 He obeyed God the Father by dying a horrible death that only bad guys got back in the day on a Roman cross.

2:9 After that, God raised him up from the grave and made him the most famous person in the universe with all the respect he deserves. Jesus' name is greater than any name in the world!

2:10 Someday, everyone in heaven and earth is going to bow down to King Jesus.

2:11 And everyone will finally admit that Jesus is in charge of everything and recognize the importance of God the Father too.

QUESTION ?

Why is Jesus the most important person
in the universe? (Vs. 5-11)

2:12 You listened well and obeyed what I said when we were together. But being apart from each other now makes it even more important that you live like Jesus wants you to, obeying him with awe and respect.

2:13 God is doing something great inside your hearts and minds; he is helping you *want* to obey him and giving you the ability to do what he wants.

QUESTION ?

Since obeying God is so hard, what does God promise to help us live for him well? (Vs. 13)

2:14 Don't argue and complain like everyone else around you.

2:15 Don't give anyone a reason to say that your faith in Jesus isn't real.

Live a life that shines the light of Hope in Jesus so brightly that it looks completely different from the lives of people who love evil darkness instead.

2:16 You can trust the Bible; stay confident in the Truth it gives you. Then, when Jesus comes back to restore everything, I will know that my life's work wasn't pointless.

2:17 But even if the Roman Emperor Nero has me killed for following Jesus, my life will be an offering that makes God glad. And I want to share that blessing with all of you!

2:18 Be happy because of Jesus, and I will share your excitement too.

2:19 Hopefully I can send Timothy to visit you soon. Then he will cheer me up when he comes back and tells me how all of you are doing in Philippi.

QUESTION ❓

Why did Paul think so highly of Timothy and Epaphroditus? (Vs. 19-30)

2:20 Timothy is awesome because he cares so deeply for all of you.

2:21 Most people around us only care about themselves instead of what Jesus cares about.

2:22 But Timothy is different than them. He's my totally trustworthy, spiritual son who has a proven track record of faithfully living and sharing the Good News of Jesus.

2:23 As soon as we learn more about what my future holds, I want to send him your way.

2:24 In fact, I think God will let me come see you myself.

2:25 Before that happens, I asked Epaphroditus to go back to you. He's amazing – a great teammate and soldier for Jesus alongside me. He helped me when I needed it most.

2:26 Epaphroditus misses you so much, and he felt badly that you heard he got sick.

2:27 And he got *really* sick – so sick that he almost died! But God was good and kept Epaphroditus alive. This was good news for me just as much as it was good news for him.

2:28 I'm really excited to send him back to you because I know you'll love being together again.

2:29 Throw Epaphroditus the biggest party you can so that he knows how much he means to you and how much you respect him as a spiritual hero.

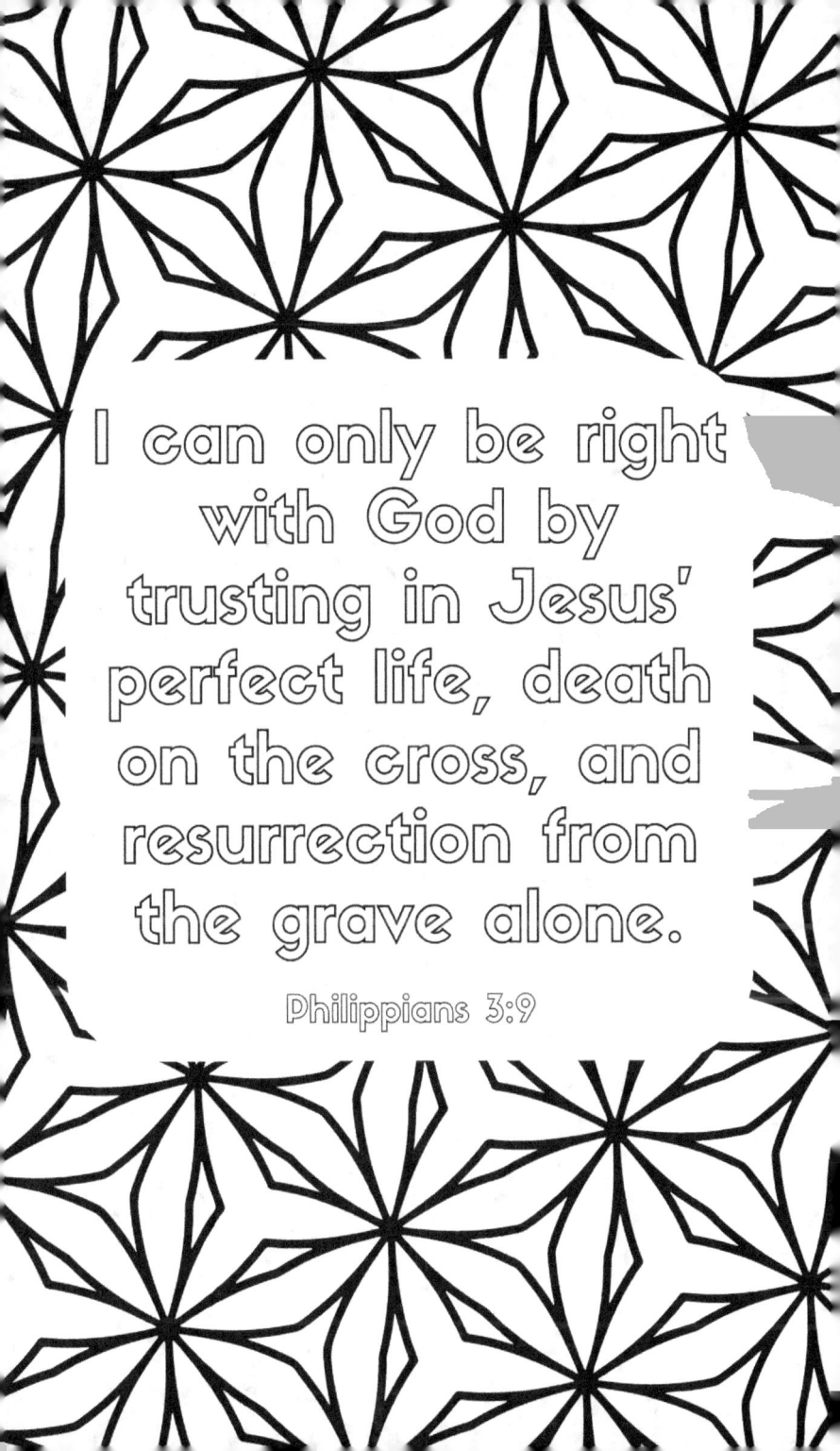

I can only be right with God by trusting in Jesus' perfect life, death on the cross, and resurrection from the grave alone.

Philippians 3:9

CHAPTER
3

3:1 But whether Emperor Nero kills me or not, keep enjoying your relationship with Jesus.

I love reminding you about this, and I keep saying it over and over so that your faith stays safe.

3:2 Don't listen to those bad guys, those false teachers who say that you need to obey rules in order to have a relationship with God. They're lying to you!

3:3 We know we have a relationship with God for two reasons:

First, we have the Holy Spirit (God living inside us) because we believe in Jesus.

Second, we only trust what Jesus did for us rather than what we do for him.

3:4 We don't trust in ourselves or how "good" we can be for God. If anyone thinks they can get to God just by doing good things, my past life would make them look silly.

QUESTION ?

How do we know that we are "saved" (that we have a real relationship with Jesus)? (Vs. 3-4)

3:5 If being a perfectly good, religious person was an Olympic sport, I'd win the gold medal every time!

I did everything that the Jewish religion said I should do. Everyone respected my family heritage the most. I was also one of the top Jewish religious leaders who obeyed all the rules (and even the extra rules that they made up).

3:6 I followed the Jewish religion so passionately that I used to hate and hurt people who followed Jesus. No one could accuse me of being a bad Jew.

3:7 I used to think trusting in myself and all my good works was worth it.

But now, I know that all my moral accomplishments

don't mean anything because King Jesus did what I could never do.

3:8 Nothing in this life means more than my relationship with Jesus. Everything in my life that I used to think mattered more than Jesus is like trash to me now.

Because Jesus means so much to me, I don't care about all the other stuff anymore.

Trying to impress God and others doesn't matter to me now.

3:9 Staying close to Jesus is the only thing I'm fighting for. I don't keep score on obeying the rules because I know God saved me by believing in Jesus. That's it.

QUESTION ❓

Is Christianity just about trying to "be really good," or is it believing that Jesus was perfectly good for us? (Vs. 8-9)

I can only be right with God by trusting in Jesus' perfect life, death on the cross, and resurrection from the grave alone.

3:10 I want to experience Jesus and his power over death. I'm even up for the hard times with Jesus that come from dying to myself and all this short life has to offer.

3:11 No matter what it takes, I know that I will beat death and come alive again through the power of Jesus alone!

3:12 Don't get me wrong; I'm not saying that I'm perfect, but I am chasing after the wholeness that Jesus offers through his sacrifice for me.

3:13 I know I'm not perfect, but I focus on where God is taking me more than I focus on my past. I look forward more than I look backward.

3:14 I'm running hard to win the race of life by trusting Jesus more and more every day. He will reward me with a never-ending prize that God's called me to win.

3:15 If you are growing in your faith and wisdom, then you should agree on what I'm teaching you. If you don't agree, then God will help you make sense of all this.

3:16 Don't back-track on how far we've already gone on this journey with Jesus!

3:17 Loved ones, please live your life imitating people who love Christ (like I do, and others too).

3:18 I'm writing with tears in my eyes right now, reminding you again to watch out for those people who hate Jesus.

3:19 Their future is only death. They only live for what they want, they brag about awful things, and they only care about what's here and now.

3:20 But we are different! Our home is Heaven (where Jesus is), and we are members of a never-ending Kingdom ruled by Christ our Lord.

3:21 He will fix our broken bodies and transform them into perfect, never-ending bodies (just like his) through the strongest power in the universe: God's power! One day Jesus will use this power to make sure everything is under his control forever.

QUESTION?

Why will the New Heaven & New Earth be awesome for those who give their lives to Jesus? (Vs. 20-21)

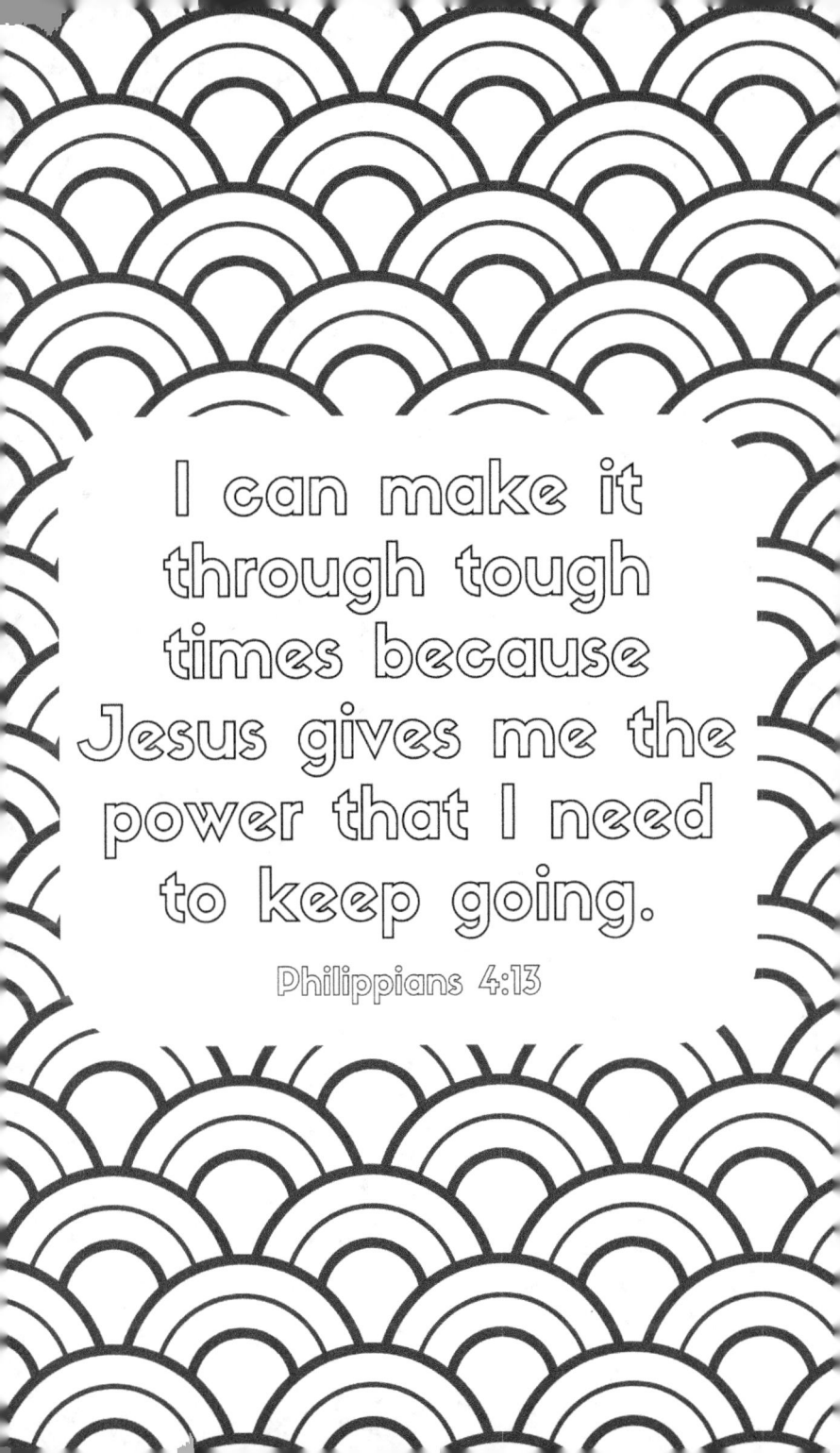

I can make it through tough times because Jesus gives me the power that I need to keep going.

Philippians 4:13

CHAPTER
4

4:1 Because of all this, fam, stay committed to Jesus. I love you lots, and I want to see you again because you are my amazing friends, you make me happy, and you are the ultimate reward I will get for all my hard work.

4:2 To my spiritual sisters Euodia and Syntyche, please start getting along and stop fighting! Please forgive each other and agree with each other.

QUESTION ?

Who is someone that you have a hard time getting along with? Who is someone you need to forgive? (Vs. 2)

4:3 And Syzygus, please help our sisters figure this out. They're teammates for Jesus with us in sharing the Hope of Jesus. Euodia and Syntyche worked with Clement and the rest of our team who are heading for Heaven together.

4:4 Stay happy because of Jesus. I'll say it again, choose joy!

4:5 Make sure everyone around you sees your love in everything you do because Jesus is coming back soon.

4:6 Don't waste time worrying about anything; instead, talk to God about everything. Share your needs with God and thank him for all he's done for you.

QUESTION ?

What is something you're worried about right now? Have you been talking to God about it?
(Vs. 6)

4:7 When you do this, God will give you peace. This supernatural stability is so great that we can't figure it out fully. God's peace will keep your hearts and minds safe as you follow Jesus.

4:8 Here's one last thing: choose to think thoughts that are true, noble, right, pure, beautiful and respectable. Choose to think about things that are awesome and worth clapping for.

QUESTION ❓

What are some things that we should clap for? Would God clap for those things? (Vs. 8)

4:9 Keep doing what you learned from me – all the stuff you heard from me and watched me do, and our peaceful God will be with you.

4:10 I'm thanking God that you care about me. Because we're so far apart, you weren't always able to help me as much as you wanted to.

4:11 I've always had what I need, and I've learned to be ok with what I have.

4:12 This is a gift from God called contentment: it means that I'm ok in every situation life throws my way.

I've learned the secret of how to keep a good attitude whether I'm hungry or full, whether I have a lot or a little.

I've learned to focus on what I do get and forget what I don't get.

QUESTION ?

Why is it so hard to "focus on what you do get and forget what you don't get?" (Vs. 12)

4:13 I can make it through tough times because Jesus gives me the power that I need to keep going.

4:14 And I'm really proud of you for sharing my pain with me.

4:15 You Philippians were the only ones who gave me money when I shared the Hope of Jesus with you and then traveled to Macedonia. No one else did what you did for me!

4:16 Even when I went to Thessalonica, you kept sending me help several times.

4:17 I'm not trying to get more money from you guys. Instead, you all deserve a prize for being so kind to me.

4:18 Right now I have more than I need from everything you sent me with Epaphroditus. Your support for me makes God really happy.

4:19 God will take care of you just like he keeps taking care of me through his never-ending supply of blessings in Jesus.

4:20 God gets all the props forever and ever!

4:21 Please tell everyone who follows Jesus there how much I love them and how much their brothers here with me love them too.

4:22 And everyone else who follows Jesus says "Hi!", including those who live with Caesar.

4:23 God is *with* you and *for* you!

CHAPTER 1

Who is a friend or family member that you can pray for today like Paul prayed for the Philippians? (Vs. 4-5, 9)

_____

_____

_____

_____

_____

What does it mean to do "the next right thing?" How will you do that today or this week? (Vs. 10)

_____

_____

_____

_____

_____

_____

Who is a friend or family member that needs a relationship with Jesus? Have *you* given your life to Jesus yet? (Vs. 12-14)

_____

_____

_____

_____

_____

_____

Why was Paul not afraid to die? (Vs. 21-22, 27)

_____

_____

_____

_____

_____

_____

CHAPTER 2

Why is it so hard to "treat others like they're more important than you are?" (Vs. 3-4)

_____

_____

_____

_____

_____

_____

Why is Jesus the most important person in the universe? (Vs. 5-11)

_____

_____

_____

_____

_____

_____

Since obeying God is so hard, what does God promise to help us live for him well? (Vs. 13)

_____

_____

_____

_____

_____

_____

Why did Paul think so highly of Timothy and Epaphroditus? (Vs. 19-30)

_____

_____

_____

_____

_____

_____

CHAPTER 3

How do we know that we are "saved" (that we have a real relationship with Jesus)? (Vs. 3-4)

_____

_____

_____

_____

_____

_____

Is Christianity just about trying to "be really good," or is it believing that Jesus was perfectly good for us? (Vs. 8-9)

_____

_____

_____

_____

_____

_____

Who are some people in your life who really love Jesus and live like Jesus? (Vs. 17)

_____

_____

_____

_____

_____

_____

Why will the New Heaven & New Earth be awesome for those who give their lives to Jesus? (Vs. 20-21)

_____

_____

_____

_____

_____

_____

CHAPTER 4

Who is someone that you have a hard time getting along with? Who is someone you need to forgive? (Vs. 2)

_____

_____

_____

_____

_____

What is something you're worried about right now? Have you been talking to God about it? (Vs. 6)

_____

_____

_____

_____

_____

_____

What are some things that we should clap for? Would God clap for those things? (Vs. 8)

_____

_____

_____

_____

_____

_____

Why is it so hard to "focus on what you do get and forget what you don't get?" (Vs. 12)

_____

_____

_____

_____

_____

_____

ABOUT DAN

*D*an is a follower of Jesus, married to his best friend Joy, and father to Landon & Declan. He's the Lead Pastor of Grace Christian Fellowship in Cortland, NY and the Founder/President of Northeast Collaborative, a regional church network. He also planted Restored Church in Wilkes-Barre, PA with a great team. Dan holds a Doctor of Ministry (D.Min.) degree from Clarks Summit University where he served as an adjunct professor, and he loves playing golf and pickleball.

WHERE DO WE GO FROM HERE?

I've got *great* news for you...there are SO many more resources out there for you and your family to dive deeper into Scripture! I would encourage you to download the **YouVersion Bible App** on your phone or device or get a printed, physical copy of the Bible in one of these three actual translations: **The New Living Translation** (NLT – 8th-grade reading level), **The New International Version** (NIV – 10th-grade reading level), or **The English Standard Version** (ESV – 12th-grade reading level). There are also two more free, online resources that I'd highly recommend: **The Bible Project** on YouTube with incredible, comprehensive, and creative overview videos of the Bible, and **GotQuestions.org** where they have answered over 700,000+ faith-related questions about God, the Scriptures, and the Hope of Jesus.